Also by Donald W. Grant

Poetry

Shades of Life
Echoes of Life
Silence of Life

Non-Fiction

M.A.G.A.: Making America Go Awry

Reflections of Life

A Collection of Poems

By
Donald W. Grant

D2C Perspectives

Copyright © 2020 by
Donald W. Grant

Cover design © 2020 by Lydia Mullins
Cover Photo © 2020 by D.W. Grant

Published By D2C Perspectives
All rights reserved.

No part of this book may be reproduced in any form or by any electronic or mechanical means including information storage and retrieval systems, without permission in writing from the author. The only exception is by a reviewer, who may quote short excerpts in a review.

ISBN: 978-1-943142-55-2
eBook: 978-1-943142-56-9

Table of Contents

Introduction
Reflection   1
Self Reflection   2
Sleep   3
Meditation   5
Journal   6
The Lady On the Veranda   7
My Roof Deck   9
The Stare   11
The Cat In the Tree   12
Spinkie-Den   13
Silver Oak   14
The Centerpiece   15
Do You Take   17
Bootcamp   18
Army Men   19
Ketchup   21
Road Trip   22
The Bully   23
The Death of My Father   25
Death   27
Unrepentant   29
Grace   30
Love   31

Just   32
Sound   33
Conundrum   34
Back   35
The Gate   36
Starfish   37
Magpies   38
Debunking Roses   40
The Concrete Ship   41
The Concrete (Not Cement Ship)   42
The Octopus   44
The Game   46
The Room   47
The Internet   49
Firestorm   50
The Burka   51
My Country   52
Division   53
God Is Pro-Choice   55
Twas the Night Before Impeachment   57
The Hypocrites   59
Our Prayer   60
In Christ?   61
A Light Into the Darkness   62
Words Can't Capture   63

Introduction

Reflections of Life is simply my intent to put on paper what I observe around me. Beginning with the poem, *Reflection*, I look at life through a philosophical lens. With the *Lady On The Veranda*, my poems take on a lighter side and less severe approach to life. My past is revealed with the section starting with *Bootcamp*. These are the hardest to write as they bring up memories best left buried. *Grace*, begins a series of poems using words that have come to me over time and poems that are a result of observing the things around me. The last section, beginning with *Firestorm*, is political. We live in a time of division and misinformation, and a time when intelligent discussions are hard as both sides of any issue dig in. You may not agree with my views, but all I ask is hopefully these poems will cause you to think. So I will leave you with this quote from John F. Kennedy:

"When power leads man to arrogance, poetry reminds him of his limitations. When power narrows the area of man's concern, poetry reminds him of the richness and diversity of existence. When power corrupts, poetry cleanses."

D. W. Grant

Reflection

Standing in front
Of the bathroom mirror
    I wonder who that is looking back.
As the brush
Scrubs at my teeth
    I see glimpses of my mother.
As the razor
Glides across my skin
    I see glimpses of my father.
The reflection I see
Looks nothing like the man
    I think I am.
The man in the mirror
Is old, gray, and thin
    Not the man I feel I am.
As I stare
And the reflection stares back,
    I ask, "Who are you?"

My mind answers

Self Reflection

Esther channels Abraham to spout the Law of Attraction
Dr. Joe tells us we need to feel the emotion
Elrod says faith must be followed by action
My mind is swirling with all this commotion

Not to confuse things with religion
But Jesus said, "Seek and ye shall find."
So, I guess the ultimate decision
Is who will I let control my mind

All this rhetoric and confusing philosophy
Really boils down to what will make me happy

The bottom line is I must take control
After all, it is my soul that I need to make whole

So believing it is up to me to visualize
The life I want to see
I have come to realize
In truth, it is just up to me.

Sleep

Sleep,
Deep sleep
Immobile through the night

Slumber,
Sound slumber,
Moving from dark to light

Time,
Time standing still
Although the clock ticks on

Portal,
A door to tomorrow
As I move from dark to dawn

Einstein,
Time is relative
A genius who knew

Asleep,
In a flash
The night is through

Clock
Moves forward
As I lie unaware

Dreams
Are all I know
As I lay without a care

Memory
Cannot recall
Details of my dream

Unless
It is a bad one
And I awake with a scream

Sadly
As night progresses
Of my rest I am clueless

Oh
To be mindful
Of the night no less

Alas
It was not meant to be

Meditation

To meditate one needs to be still
To shut out the world, to concentrate

No matter how quiet one gets, there
Are always thoughts way back that irritate

To meditate one needs to breathe very slowly
One needs to focus on each breath, as you breathe deep

Maybe those thoughts you can't eliminate
Are there so you don't go so deep you fall asleep.

Journal

Secret thoughts, emotions
Not meant to be shown.

Written with hesitation
Words that are mine alone.

Pages filled over time
A record of life sped by.

Feelings caught up in ink
Some very low, some high

A notebook full,
Ready to be locked away.

If others eyes could see.
I wonder, "What would they say?"

The Lady On the Veranda

She had been lured out by the warmth of the sun,
Shining cloud free on a lazy Saturday afternoon.
Elegantly posed in a plastic green patio chair,
She sat eating the last of her orzo with feta cheese.

She had added a small dab of coleslaw to offset
The tartness of her favorite midday snack.
As she set her Calvin Klein plate down beside her chair,
The sun reflected off her auburn hair,
Highlighting the almost blond streaks it had caused
from her previous outings.

Her long legs were accented by her Neiman-Marcus sandals,
And her toe ring hinted at a little bit of her wild side.
Her shoulders and arms were tanned and stood sensuous
Against her blue sleeveless top from Bloomingdales.

She reached for her bottle of Samuel Adams to cool her throat
And quench the thirst the orzo had brought on.
In her right hand was a small cigar, Cuban,
That she gently puffed, just enough to keep it lit.

As the smoke lifted from her, she set the beer to the side,
Replacing it with a ripe cherry from the bowl she had
Brought into the sunshine. She enjoyed working the fruit
From around the pit as the cherry turned over in her mouth.
Swallowing the delicious fruit, she was now left with the pit.

Turning her head slightly, she spit the pit.
It traveled about six feet hitting the fence post
With a ricocheting effect and sound to match.
The pit sailed over the fence careening off the forehead
Of her neighbor as he stood watering his plants.

"Sorry," she yelled, leaning down to get another sip of beer,
As the cigar smoke curled skyward toward the sun
That had brought the lady to the veranda.

My Roof Deck

As I sit on my roof deck
I can ponder the world
A world full of wonder and amazement

From the pair of doves
Cooing as they sit on the wire
To the sound of a plane streaking overhead

A crow, blacker than the darkest night
Moves from tree to tree
Searching for what, I do not know

There is a large black bee
That flitters from opening to
Opening along the rail looking
For a place to hide

Not sure where it is but
I can see the thin strings
Of a spider web running from the roof
Across the skylight

The sound of the waves
Reaches my ears, melodic,
Soothing my soul

The peace I feel is enhanced
By the cigar smoke curling
Above my head, as I sip
A cool glass of white wine.

The Stare

Her eyes lock on like
Radar grabbing a target.
Laser like, she stares.

If she were not her
One might think her
Mind is just daydreaming.

If she were not her
One might perceive her
As just contemplating life.

If she were not her
One might say she
Is perplexed, confused.

If only we could ask her,
"Are you daydreaming,
Contemplating, perplexed."

But she is herself
And like the stare of an infant
We will never know what the cat sees.

The Cat In the Tree

Normally a cat in a tree
Would be a terrible thing,
Stuck high above ground
Scared, alone and unreachable.

Usually firemen would be called
A truck and ladder brought to the scene
The hero would rescue the cat
The crowd would be clapping with glee.

But here there are two cats in a tree
A tree not of branches and wood
Lounging in my living room on
A tree of cloth and hemp

A tree that is not really a tree.

Spinkie-Den

As I emerged from the forest
I came to a clearing full of flowers

As far as my eye could see
Blossoms rose from the earth

The sun made them into gold
Dazzling and bright to my eyes

I thought what a pleasant place to be
When a voice from a distant past came to me

The voice had a lilt, a Scottish sound,
An ancestor of mine from long ago

What ye see now, way back when
We simply called a Spinkie-Den.

Silver Oak

The bottle sits in a rack of three
Empty now, but kept for the memory
A Cab along with a Zin and a Chablis.

The rack is wrought iron from a small boutique
The label on the wine makes the bottle unique
Aged to perfection, corked at its peek.

We have been to the vintner, an overnight trip
Napa Valley, from where the wine is shipped.
To test this vintage, a glass to our lips.

Of all we have tasted, the is the finest
We drink it ourselves, never with guests,
For special occasions, this is the best.

Anniversaries and birthdays, come and they go
One thing we can count on, one thing that we know,
Is Silver Oak Cabernet costs a lot of dough!

The Centerpiece

It was equidistant from all sides
A beautiful array of potpourri.
Spiraling away from this masterpiece
Candelabras, water and wine goblets,
Handmade turkeys with names attached.

Plates evenly spread, silverware put
On the proper sides. Emily Post beamed.
The food began to appear, cranberry sauce
Turkey, and gravy in a proper boat,
Baked spaghetti a family tradition.

The table was full, everyone properly placed
When out came one more platter full of
Cut carrots, olives, and celery with
No room for it to land.

The son-in-law reached for the center piece
Politely making room.
The table went quiet, everyone afraid to breathe
The sound came with a tone that chilled.

One would have thought it was Indiana Jones
Lifting the artifact in Raiders of the Lost Ark
Causing the stone to roll, causing
Harrison Ford to run for his life.

This was not a stone but the threat was as real
The matriarch stated as serious as death,
"Do not touch that!"

Do You Take...

Over the years many I have wed,
Not me personally, but with words that I have said,
Officially officiating many ceremonies.
By law the only question needing to be asked
"Do you Take…?" Legally my only task.
Once answered, husband and wife now bound in matrimony

What few ever hear as vows they make
Is the meaning of the words that each other take.
So I try to share the origins in every ceremony.

You see, husband is a word that comes from a band
That wraps around a barrel so pressure it can stand,
Holding a marriage together like wine held for aging.

As the pressure of life begins to unfold
It's the husband with strength a marriage to hold,
In love and respect, to him not a duty.

Wife has its roots in a word that means trellis
Giving direction and guidance amid all the hustle,
Making sure thru all the marriage lies stability.

So next time you find yourself at a wedding,
Remember these words as the couple is uniting.

Bootcamp

We came from California, young
And raw, to Fort Polk Louisiana.
Arriving by bus and dumped out onto
Hot pavement, told to line up and shut up.

The drill sergeant with his Smokey-the-Bear hat
Looked us over one by one, his voice harsh
And his eyes cold as stone, looking
For any reason to dress us down.

He came to me and his face froze.
"What is that on your face, boy?"
"Peach fuzz?" I sheepishly answered.
"What do you use to shave with son," he barked.
" My electric razor." I said. Then adding, "Sir."
"Where are you going to plug that in when
You are in the middle of the jungle in 'Nam?"
Pausing I said, "It's rechargeable sir."
His face went red, the veins popping out,

His eyes on fire as he screamed,
"In this man's Army you shave every day,
You shave with a razor like a man."
It was with this introduction my Army time began.

Army Men

One has a radio, calling for help
One on the ground, rifle at the ready
One is in a beret, special forces maybe
The scariest of all holding a machine gun

As a team, they are protecting a Jeep
The workhorse that won World War II
Mine is more modern, not olive drab
But black with amenities they never had

The men and the Jeep displayed on a shelf
All but the Jeep found along the sea
Toy soldiers left by children at play
Each one bringing back my childhood memory

When I was a kid these same soldiers I had
Model planes and tanks, and ships that I made
We built them with Revelle glue and always inside
We added to each a little surprise

We would play war with these little men
With planes from the sky and tanks on the ground
We pretended it was real, and just to be sure
We covered them in lighter fluid and watched as they blew

For extra effect our little surprise
Was the firecracker we had placed on the inside
So as our imaginations were fueled
Our little war was too.

Ketchup

The bottle stood in the center
Equidistant from both our arms
The meatloaf warm, needing just a splash.

My sister reached for it as did I
Our hands grasping either side
She would not let go, nor would I

My father never spoke a word
It was his arm that hit my chest
With no air to breathe, I simply collapsed.

The meatloaf was warm against my face
My sister, this time, was triumphant
My mother spoke what would become my fate.

"Don't ever touch him again!"

Road Trip

The road seemed to be endless
Hours of motion, the horizon never closer
My nine year old mind wandering.

The station wagon was brand new
Back then restraints non existent
My sister and I loose in the very back.

As the miles swept by periodically my father
Would pull to the side of the road
A sound, a hiss, maybe a leak?

Four times we stopped, then off again
Only to to stop once more, making it five.
What sound had his ear detected?

With a glance in the rear view mirror, he saw
Me in the back with a corn cob pipe
Mindlessly blowing
Periodically.

The Bully

Being the new kid was never a problem for me
My dad was military so moving was what I was used to

Every few years we packed up and moved
It was just something we knew we had to do

He retired just before I was to start high school
Which meant we were finally in one place

The beauty of starting over means at each new
Place one can renew oneself, put on a new face

The first week of school I had not made any friends
But at the end of the week there was a school dance

In fourth grade I had won a bop contest
So, I looked at the dance as here is my chance

Before I had even reached the door, a senior
Confronted me and asked if I was new

I said yes and he said
This is what you are going to do

Go on inside and sit in the bleachers
Don't talk to anyone, especially a teacher

If I see you move before it's over
You might be leaving here in an ambulance

So that was my intro to high school
And how I experienced my first dance

To this day my only regret was not standing
Up to this punk, and saying, "You want to bet!"

The Death of My Father

My father died at the age of sixty-two
I believe it was nineteen-seventy-eight
Maybe there is a reason I don't remember the exact date

Elisa Matvejeva said she was never enough
For not only her mother, but her father too.
Never enough for my father, was how I felt too.

My father died of cancer you see
Melanoma that had been misdiagnosed
Not being there at the end, the thing I hate most

There were words left unspoken, to my regret
Words had I been there, that I would have said
My words and my feelings came after he was dead

My mother asked if I would do the eulogy
Before we could have a memorial service
There were a couple of things we had to do first

The mortuary where he was supposed to be
Called to say he had not been delivered yet
The body still at the hospital, the one for Vets.

So my uncle and I went down to see
If we could figure why he wasn't where he was
supposed to be
The morgue said they still had the body so
It was left up to me to go down and see

Sure enough there he was, his body on a gurney
Waiting to be taken to the mortuary
I made sure he was delivered and delivered the eulogy

When all this was over, I still had regrets
Like I have said of the words never spoken
With nothing else left but time to mourn

Today the only thing left as far as a memory
Is the feeling that he made my life tough
Although he is gone, I know I was never enough.

(Note: Elisa Matvejeva is a poet and her poem "I Was Never Enough" from her book *Flowers I Should Have Thrown Away Yesterday*, inspired this one.)

Death

What is death?
What happens when you die?

Is it the end
Or the beginning?

A blackness of nothing
Or a glorious light?

Or are we just memories
Projected on the ones we leave behind?

At our last breath
Whom do we meet?

The grim reaper
In black with his scythe

Charon the ferryman
Across the river Styx

Loved ones lost
Ever so long ago

Anubis, jackal like
As we await judgement

What happens when we die?
One of the best responses I have heard

From Keanu Reeves, yes
From Neo himself

"I know the ones we leave
Will miss us."

Unrepentant

The priest quietly entered the room
His hand holding the pyx.
The man lying in the bed
Oblivious to the new presence.

The man was staring at
What only he could see
The priest came to the bed
Putting his hand on the man's

"I came to give the Eucharist"
The priest said in a whisper
The man did not move
His eyes still locked on some unknown

Before the priest could speak again
The man turned his head
His eyes locked on the priests
"Go to hell," he said.

The man turned away.

Grace

Is a word that can be amazing
A forgiveness from God if the Bible is true

It can be given as a name to smile to
And if modified used as in Gracie Allen

Okay so for some a name too old, the wife of George Burns
So let us use one more familiar as in Grace Slick

It can be described as a woman of poise
A woman brought up to be refined

Or a nom de plume for royalty
When one does not use your highness

But my favorite use of this lovely word
Is when I see someone stumble or trip

And as they regain their poise I say
"Way to go, Grace."

My wife hates this!

Love

Love, to see it in myself,
See it in others
Is the intention of Love.

Just

Just
A word only text can define
With bust, must, or gust
So easy to make it rhyme.

Just
Wait a minute one could say
If one just needed a pause
Time just to think or delay

Just
Could be exactly or absolutely
As just what I need.
You hit the nail on the head, precisely.

But for me and I would agree
With Chekhov that the main thing
Is to be just -
    If a better world we want to see.

Sound

The City
Honks
Curses
Whistles
Rattles
Cacophony

The Suburbs
Mower
"You're safe"
"Fore"
"Dinner"
Symphony

The Country
Brook
Birds
Wind
Laughter
Serenity

Conundrum

When does the pupil of the eye
Become the pupil seeing the teacher

Should we really be making a game
Out of sport hunting, hunting game

Why when we outlaw something
If you do it you are an outlaw

We knead dough when making bread
But we need dough, also bread

Once I read a book, is it
Okay to ask if you have read it too

Pondering all this can make one blue
But then isn't the sky blue too.

Back

The human body is complex and amazing
With the mind and extraordinary effort
One can accomplish anything

We don't need to think to breathe, to take
One step in front of the other as we
Walk around the lake

We can hurt ourselves and heal fast
New growth springs to life
Repairing what happened in the past

As complex and amazing
As our bodies can be
I don't understand one thing

How can a slight twitch in our back
Drop us to our knees in pain
Leave us immobile, flat on our back?

The Gate

The mighty redwood gave its life
So I could feel secure.
Shaped thin and long to be
Formed by blade and lathe.

Now spanning the gap
Between house and fence
A barrier, a warning
Not to intrude.

But the enemy came unseen
Not a man nor beast.
But a fiend ready to destroy
The mighty redwood from within.

Slowly, determined, not one
But a swarm,
Termites.

Starfish

They call me a Starfish.
Which is a little odd
As I am not a star,
Nor a fish.

I guess if you use your imagination,
I could look like a star,
I could look like a fish.
But, in truth, I am just a Crustacean.

While I call my home the sea,
It seems there, I was not meant to be.
For as much as home I would like it to call,
You are more likely to find me,
Adorning a wall.

Magpies

Heckle and Jeckle they were not
But they easily could have been

At first they were shy, a bit afraid
But as they days progressed all fear was lost

Raw meat was what did the trick
Each toss bringing them ever closer

But then what we did not expect
Had we thought we would have known

Each day we fed them around three
They might not talk but they knew

Each day at three they suddenly appeared
Landing on the porch coming near the door

Now a magpie can sing, a very pleasant sound
But they can also screech, not a pleasant sound

To let us know it was time to be fed
They did not sing, that would have been nice

No, they screeched until with meat we appeared
Now unafraid almost coming into the house

Now the sad end to this little tale of ours
Is that we were visitors to this small shire

Leaving, we left our hosts with new friends.

Debunking Roses

Roses are not just red,
I've seen yellow, white, black
And even blue.

Violets are blue but
Also yellow, white and,
Of course, violet too.

Sugar, as we all know is sweet,
Especially if you have a cavity
Or two.

And as to the you,
As Carol Muske would say,
"You who?"

So while this isn't really a poem,
Although it has been used as such,
A true poet would say,
"Not so much!"

The Concrete Ship

Storms have taken their toll
Now she lies twisted and bent

Once a carrier of dance and laughter
Now a refuge for seal and otter

Birds now stand where passengers could
Leaving their droppings to rot and smell

She had been built for war
But was created too late.

Towed to shore, she sits
No battle will she ever see.

Some call her an eyesore
For others she holds a meaning

Some believe she may be haunted
Others wish she would cease to be.

For now she remains as a tribute
To the ingenuity of man.

The concrete ship now
Forever, bound to the sand.

The Concrete (Not Cement) Ship

She sits alone, broken
Once created by the ingenuity of man,
Once created for man's stupidity.

Never given a chance
To fulfill her purpose,
Destined for man's frivolity

Nature has not been kind to her
Sending wave and wind to keep her
From being used for man's sins

Man had such grandiose plans for her
Dinner and dancing and gambling
Even some bootleg gin

The strain was too much
And she began to crack
Her time of pleasure short-lived

So, stripped to the bone
Her only attraction, becoming
A place for the sea to give
Up its bounty 'til at last
She broke even more, now
Only web feet move across her deck

Otters and seals swim thru her bowels
Often getting caught up in
Her re-bar by the neck

Her decay grows day by day
And her body is clothed in feculence
Her odor, at times, intolerable.

For all she has been through
Maybe her biggest shame
Is for people to not even to
Know her correct name

She was christened
The USS Palo Alto
One of several concrete ships
But people mistakenly refer to her

As The Cement Ship.

The Octopus

It is a creature framed
From tales of yore

It is a monster, a deep sea terror
A legend found in folklore

Novel and film have depicted it to be
Gigantic, from Jules Verne to
"It Came From Beneath the Sea."

In reality the octopus is more
Like you and like me

It has nine brains, one in each arm,
One in its head

That is eight more than us and
Eight and a half more than some

It has three hearts, two more than us
And again, three more than some

A fascinating creature highly intelligent
Able to camouflage itself
Aware, always vigilant.

A delicacy to some, for others a thing
Not to be eaten

Regardless of how you feel, I hope
In the sea to never greet one.

The Game

First steps taken as those
Watching wait for you to falter
Moving down the path ahead
Having to veer to the side

What you do and how you react
Becomes a matter of pride
There will always be those
Better than you
Yet you never give up

Disappointment will come
But a small triumph means more
Your mind sees the path
Your body does not always agree

In the end you look back
If only, what if
Alas it was not meant to be
Yet you try again, renewed
With hope, this time
Will be better

The Room

She sits confined to her chair
With a door that has no lock
A door made of glass so those
Without can see within
And she never feels really alone

Misogynists are slain by her
Ever wielding sword
Ghosts are drawn to her hoping
She will release them to the next plane

Neighbors come to her sharing
Their secrets
Mothers seek her help in
Protecting their own

Those buried by debt seek
Her advice to reclaim their life
Women striving to get ahead
Seek her wisdom only to be told
Climbing the ladder can be murder

Those oppressed by religious tenets
Call to her for salvation
Seeking the freedom she enjoys

Strangers are welcomed but
Need to understand
She knows their secrets

Her sword is her pen
And from her room she
Decides the fate of the world,

The Internet

The tool that was meant to
Give us the truth
Has become that which we
Cannot believe is truth

Firestorm

The fire blazes fed by the wind
Heat unbearable backing off the firemen
Trees aflame, brush on fire
In its push lives lost upon the pyre

Dwellings fall, possessions lost
Destruction mounts, Oh the cost
Flames begun not by careless thought
But by greed has the chaos wrought

By years of neglect, ignoring the signs
This nightmare exists almost by design
Corporate greed, concern for the bottom line
Telling the rest of us, all is fine

Now confronted with the truth, public outrage
Their solution is to hand us a power outage
So not only is it land and homes that are gone
But jobs and products when no power is on

Enough is enough, it is time that we see
Accountability and fines demanded from PG&E.

(Note: For non-Californians that is Pacific Gas and Electricity)

The Burka

Hair, not wanting to be seen
Ears, mouth, lips concealed

Arms and legs covered
As little as possible being revealed

Yet, the eyes
Said to be the window to the soul
Used to acknowledge, or at
Disbelief, to roll

Orbs that seductively pull you
From across a crowded room
Able to express what she intends

Beautiful sirens holding one transfixed
Making sure you pay attention
And with a gaze the truth unmixed

For the eyes have all the power
To love or to hate
They can smile, or worse, glower

So, it has always seemed strange to me
That the most seductive part of the face
Is the only part they let you see.

My Country

My country 'tis of thee, no longer do I feel free
My country 'tis of thee, feels like we have lost our democracy
My country 'tis of thee, what happened to liberty?
My country 'tis of thee, now with a polluted sea
My country 'tis of thee, a divided land I now see
My country 'tis of thee, with skies unfit for you and me
My country 'tis of thee, this is not what you are supposed to be.

Division

"In the beginning, God."
Was the last time there was unity
The first split came as that which is in heaven
Was separated from that which is earth.

Then came the division of dark and light
The day now opposite of the night

Creatures were then formed, some
On the land, some in the sea
Man was created last and given
Reign over all that was meant to be

Out of man, woman was born, and
Is there not greater division than
Between a woman and man?

Brothers became jealous, so
Abel was killed by Cain
The first murder, but not the last
Over cattle and grain.

It seems from the beginning
Division would be never ending

The inhabitants of this planet have
Always found ways to divide
Be it language, race, religion, or
Politics, someone always on the opposite side

Imagine all the world as one,
As once envisioned by Lennon

So as it was in the beginning
It shall be in the end
After man no longer on this earth trods
Unity will return, there will be just God.

God Is Pro-Choice

God has created all that there is
Choose another name, the Universe,
Allah, Higher power, Creator
What you call God does not matter

for as creations man and woman
have been given a choice

In the beginning the choice was
obey or taste the forbidden fruit
A choice that meant giving up paradise

Man, and here we mean generic
for all, made a choice to leave

Throughout time God has allowed
The human race to choose.

To believe or not
To follow or not
To obey or not
To love or not
To live or not

God, who could have never given us
A choice, created evil,
An ulcer in the body of Christ .

So that we, above all of creation
Could choose.

Twas the Night Before Impeachment

'Twas the night before impeachment, when all through the White House
Not a politician was stirring, except Steve Miller, the louse.
The wall was being built by money stolen from the Pentagon
In hopes that all the brown skinned immigrants would soon be gone.

Trump's children were nestled all snug in their beds
While visions of profits danced in their heads
And Melania in her own room, and Trump a floor above
Poor Baron asleep, whom no one seems to love

When out on the East lawn there arose such a clatter
The Secret Service ran out to see what was the matter
Away from the window Trump ran very fast
Forgetting everyone else, trying to save his own ass

The lights of the White House gave off a bright glow
Revealing a group on the lawn, a group we all know
More rabid than dogs, his enemies came,
Trump tweeted and tweeted calling them names

"Now Nervous Nancy! Now Little Adam Schiff!
You should be after Crooked Hillary!
Go find her emails that she cleverly hid
She is the crook, certainly it's not me

In the blink of an eye with warrants in hand
The FBI swarmed in shouting just one command
"You're under arrest Mr. President,
Put your hands in the air."
Trump cowered in a corner crying,
"Arrest *me*! You wouldn't dare."

So, they led him outside to the waiting van
Where Pompeo and Barr sat handcuffed as well
Giuliani and Pence were chained in the back
And as they drove off everyone could tell
This was the best impeachment of all
For at last we could say to these crooks,
"Farewell."

The Hypocrites

He lies
But he says Merry Christmas
He is an adulterer
But he says he's one of us!

He wants to build a wall
But only to protect us
He hates
But only those not like us

He has never read the Bible
But he calls it a fine book
He misquotes God's word
But prayers with us he took

He belittles women
But only those who do not know their place
He wants America white
After all, aren't we the superior race?

He makes false promises
But just wait and see
He is a hypocrite
But….then so are we.

Our Prayer

Our Father, assuming there is a heaven
However name you want to go by
Your kingdom is hopefully better
Than this one on earth
As it was meant to be
Give us free medical care
And forgive our student debt
Impeach those that obstruct justice
And lead them all to a cell
Deliver us from the GOP
For we want a better country
Where power goes to the people
For ever and ever.

As it is written, let it be.

In Christ?

In Christ?
Eyes that are blind to color and difference
Eyes that see possibility

In Christ?
Hands that do not put down
Hands that reach out

In Christ?
Feet that do not trod upon
Feet that move to help

In Christ?
Heart that does not hate
Heart that is open

In Christ?
Religion that is not damnation
Religion that encompasses all

In Christ?
Love, Compassion
Understanding, Equality
Hope, Peace

A Light Into the Darkness

The conflict had come to an end
The wall of division had come down
The actors had left the stage, and then
Cruel fate, unrelenting, stepped in

The tension had been released
Both sides agreed to step down
Finally, a real chance for peace
'Til the ray of hope was decreased

The feet came to a halt
The banners had been laid down
Brotherhood seemingly bought
Then again chaos was wrought

Three souls had met their end
Long ago committed to the ground
So now darkness o'er the land reigns
So only one question remains

Who will step up and put this darkness down?

Words Can't Capture

Words cannot capture the moment
When the heart quickens.
When emotions trigger and one's blood
Wildly rushes thru one's veins

No author or poet has ever
Noted the feeling, the passion
Now so intense, so consuming
No one can deny its power

The use of all this can come
Thoroughly unexpected, from
The sight of one we love or
The sound from a voice long forgotten

From the pride in a belief or
From a memory we hold
From an injustice we see or
From something unexpected

Religion can spark all of this
Racism has the power to
Release a rage within as we
Realize the cruelty it creates

Is it a song that stirs the past?
Is it perhaps just the intensity of the music?
Is it the lover of a country? Or
Is it the thought of losing it all?

What stirs a man's soul?
Where does such passion erupt?
When does it cause us to act?
Why do we wait so long?

www.ingramcontent.com/pod-product-compliance
Lightning Source LLC
Chambersburg PA
CBHW031310060426
42444CB00033B/1157